Contents

Is it an animal or a plant?

1,2

Class 2 sorted these pictures into animals and plants.

They made tables like this:

Animal	What it is like
Dog	Four legs

⭐ Do you know the difference between plants and animals? Why are you an animal?

Plant	What it is like
Daisy	Green leaves, white flower and a stem

⭐ Use Task Sheets 1 and 2 to show what you know.

Animal hunt

Class 2 went on an animal hunt around their school.
This is what they saw.

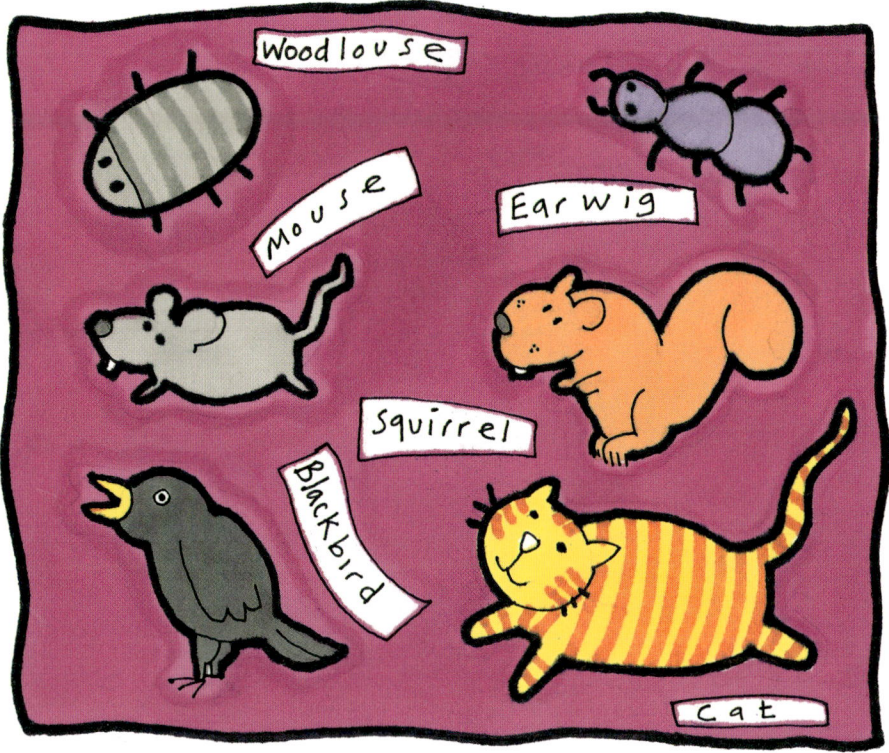

Woodlouse

Earwig

Mouse

Squirrel

Blackbird

Cat

⭐ Go on an animal hunt.

⭐ Draw or take photographs of any animals you see.

⭐ Make a class display of your pictures.

Comparing animals

Class 2 collected animal pictures from magazines. They also printed pictures using a computer.

Here are some of their animal pictures.

⭐ How are these animals like each other?

⭐ How are they different?

Caring for pets

3

Class 2 made a fact sheet about caring for pets.

My pet is a cat

My cat eats cat food

My cat drinks milk and water

My cat needs a warm, safe place to sleep

My cat has a toy mouse and ball

✷ Choose a pet.

✷ Plan and write a fact sheet about how to look after your pet. Add drawings.

✷ Use Task Sheet 3.

How people are alike

4

Class 2 thought about how they were all alike. They made a list and added drawings.

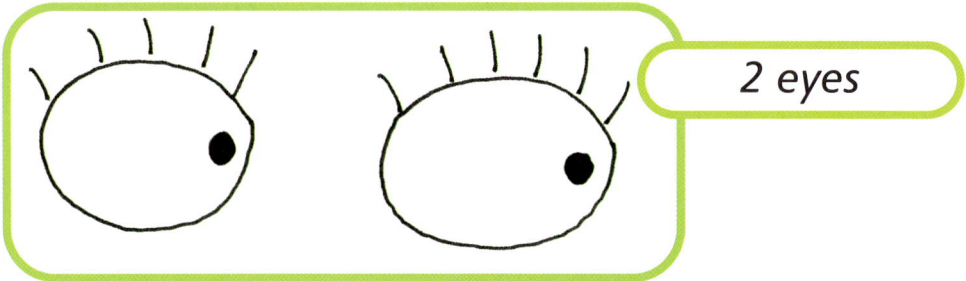

2 eyes

2 legs

⭐ List five ways in which all humans are alike.

⭐ Add a picture for each one.

⭐ Use Task Sheet 4.

Sort the photos

Class 2 brought in recent photographs.
They sorted the photos into groups.
One group sorted them like this:

black hair

brown hair

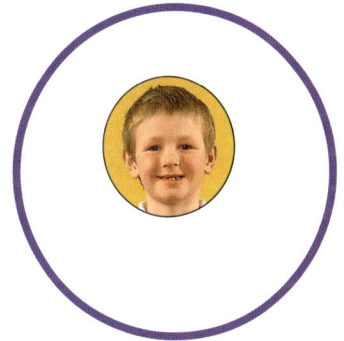

fair hair

⭐ How could you sort your photos? Try it.

⭐ Tell another group how you sorted them.

Who's who?

Maria drew a picture of her friend Anil.
Then she wrote about him.

This is Anil.
He is quite tall and thin.
He has brown eyes and
black hair. He has glasses
He is my friend.

⭐ Draw and write about another person in your class. Do not use their name.

⭐ Share your picture and writing with the class.

⭐ Ask the other children to guess who you have written about. Was your description good? How do you know?

Growing older

5

As people grow older, they change.

⭐ How will you change as you get older?

⭐ Use Task Sheet 5 to draw a picture of you as a grown-up.

⭐ How have you changed?

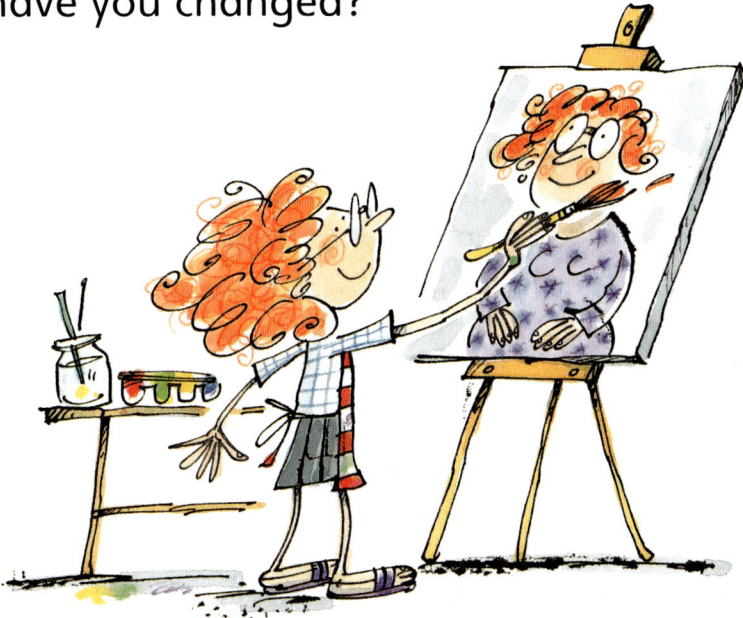

⭐ Swap your drawings. Can your friends still recognise you? Which things are different?

Measuring differences in people

6

Class 2 measured these parts of their bodies.

⭐ In your group, measure these parts of your body.

⭐ Use Task Sheet 6 to record your findings.

Task 10 **Hand spans**

7

⭐ Look again at Task Sheet 6. How do the hand spans vary?

⭐ Complete a class hand span survey.

⭐ Make a tally chart. Use Task Sheet 7.

Class survey

Name	Hand span in centimetres
Jane	11
Mark	12

Class tally chart

Hand span in centimetres	Number of children	
11	⧵⧵⧵⧵ //	7
12	///	3

11

Task 11 Making graphs

Class 2 made a block graph of their hand span results.

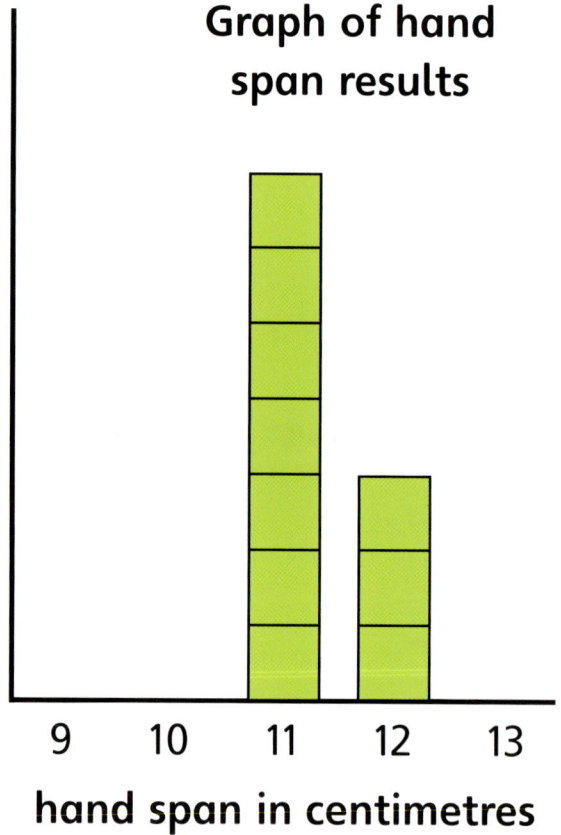

Graph of hand span results

number of children

9   10   11   12   13

hand span in centimetres

⭐ Draw a block graph of your class results.

⭐ What size hand span do most children have?

⭐ What is the smallest and biggest hand span?

Class 2 wanted to find out if people with the biggest hand span have the biggest feet.

⭐ How could you find out?

Class 2 lined up in order of shoe size, and then in order of hand span size.

Look at the two pictures.

⭐ What do they tell you?

⭐ Now try this in your class.

Plant similarities and differences

Like animals, plants have lots of differences.

⭐ Choose two plants.

⭐ Draw and label the stem, root, leaf and flower.

⭐ How are they alike? How are they different?

⭐ Make a list.

Animal spotters

8

Class 2 went for a walk. They listed and counted the animals they saw. They sorted them into animals with wings and animals with no wings.

They made a block graph.

worm   ///
moth   /
beetle ₩₩ //
spider ////
bee   //
bird   ₩₩ /

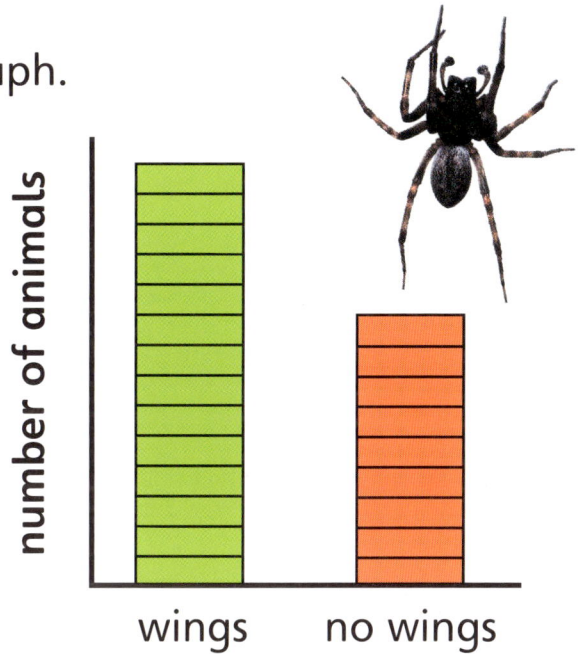

number of animals

wings   no wings

⭐ Go on another animal hunt walk.
⭐ Use Task Sheet 8 to list and count the animals you see.
⭐ How could you sort them?
⭐ Make a class block graph.

Tropical Fish

Here's a tank full of fish
Of every shape and size,
With different shaped tails and
Different coloured eyes.
But they all like to swim
And nibble at weed,
And they come to the top
When it's time for a feed.

★ How are the fish different?

★ How are they the same?